WORLDVIEW GUIDE

WAR AND PEACE

Samuel Dickison

canonpress
Moscow, Idaho

Published by Canon Press
P.O. Box 8729, Moscow, Idaho 83843
800.488.2034 | www.canonpress.com

Samuel Dickison, *Worldview Guide for War and Peace*
Copyright © 2018 by Samuel Dickison.
For the Canon Classics edition of the novel go to www.canonpress.com/books/
canon-classics.

Cover design by James Engerbretson
Cover illustration by Forrest Dickison
Interior design by Valerie Anne Bost and James Engerbretson

Printed in the United States of America.

Scripture quotations are from New King James Version®. Copyright © 1982 by
Thomas Nelson. Used by permission. All rights reserved.

A free end-of-book test and answer key are available for download at
www.canonpress.com/ClassicsQuizzes

18 19 20 21 22 23   9 8 7 6 5 4 3 2 1

CONTENTS

INTRODUCTION

There is a shelf load of great books whose mere size places them in a special category. These are the heavy hitters; slap some mortar between them and you have a respectable fortress. Of course, size by itself is no indication of greatness, but at the very least it communicates "the commitment the writer shouldered in order to create the work, the commitment [a reader] must make to digest it."[1] Leo Tolstoy's *War and Peace* is perhaps the most formidable of these books. But the most impressive thing about Tolstoy's magnum opus is that over three hundred and sixty-three chapters and well over half a million words he not only crafts a compelling story, but presents a view of life deeper and more vivid than many authors ever dream of.

---

1. Stephen King, *On Writing: A Memoir of the Craft* (New York: Scribner, 2000), 135.

THE WORLD AROUND

War and Peace was published in two main installments: the first in 1866 and the second in 1869. The mid 19th century was a stormy time for Russia. Only a few years before *War and Peace* was published, Tsar Alexander II had liberated the serfs, finally dismantling the feudal system that Europe had abandoned centuries earlier. Russia had also recently emerged from the bloody and disappointing Crimean War, a war in which Tolstoy himself fought. And, particularly relevant to Tolstoy's work, the memory of Napoleon's burning of Moscow in 1812 had not yet drifted into the foggy past.

Of course history, that many-tentacled animal, was not confined to Russia. Henry Ford and Wilbur Wright, each a world-changer in their own right, were both born in the 1860s, while Jesse James ran wild in the American West and the American East struggled to recover in the wake of the Civil War. In 1869 the business tycoon Leland

Stanford hammered the celebratory final golden spike into the Transcontinental Railroad. That same year Mohandas Gandhi, who would later be heavily influenced by Tolstoy's writing, was born in Gujarat, India. Even more importantly, America formed its first professional baseball team: the Cincinnati Red Stockings.[2]

All in all, the years surrounding the publication of *War and Peace* were transformative in many ways. Realism and the novel, a relatively new form, were taking hold in literature. Politically and technologically the world was rushing towards modernity. And yet, as Tolstoy showed, people were very much the same as they had always been.

---

2. *The Timetables of History* (New York: Touchstone, 1982) is a great resource for this kind of thing.

ABOUT THE AUTHOR

Although birth isn't a bad place to begin a biography, Leo (or Lev) Nikolayevich Tolstoy's death gives us perhaps a better introduction to who he was. In 1910, at the age of 82, he snuck out of his family home at Yasna Polyana in the middle of the night and boarded a train. He was, he explained in a letter to his wife Sonya, "going to do what people of my advanced years commonly do: withdraw from the concerns of the world in order to spend my remaining years in peace and tranquility."[3] He then asked that his wife make no attempt to follow him. Shortly after his midnight departure, Tolstoy fell ill aboard the train and was forced to get out at the station in Astapovo. He had been trailed by both a government agent and a reporter, and within a few days a hoard of newspaper men, photographers, and cinematographers had gathered

---

3. David Modell, "Tolstoy's Letters to His Wife," *North American Review* 200, no. 707 (Oct. 1914): 601.

to witness the final hours of the great Russian. He had run away to find solitude, yet here he was, the center of headlines around the world.

Tolstoy's life was full of such contrasts. He fathered thirteen children before embracing strict celibacy. He moved from hedonism to freemasonry to Russian Orthodoxy only to be excommunicated when he founded his own radical sect. He was a wealthy landlord who dressed like a peasant, a soldier turned pacifist, and a vegetarian before such diets were fashionable. Tolstoy's life was, in many ways, as broad and varied as that of his own characters.

Tolstoy was born in 1828.[4] Both his parents died when he was young and he was raised by aunts. He attended the local university and was a prolific reader, but dropped out and never graduated. He was, however, particularly impressed with Rousseau, so much so that he wore a medallion of him around his neck.[5] In his early years he drank and womanized with almost Augustinian energy until finally he joined the army to break the bad habits he had formed. He fought alongside his brother in the Crimean War and witnessed firsthand the bloody mayhem of Sevastopol.

---

4. Amy Mandelker's introduction to the Oxford / Maude edition of *War and Peace* (New York: Oxford University Press, 2010) has a lot of good biographical information on Tolstoy.

5. From the introduction to the Great Books edition of *War and Peace* (Chicago: Encyclopedia Britannica, Inc., 1952).

In 1862 he married Sonya Bhers. Not only did she bear him thirteen children (five of whom died before adulthood) but over the course of his work on *War and Peace* she copied out the manuscript by hand eight separate times.

The final decades of Tolstoy's life were marked by an increasing fanaticism. Having dabbled in freemasonry and Orthodoxy, Tolstoy finally decided that real truth lay in his own unique interpretation of the Gospels. He rejected the institutional Church (and was excommunicated in 1901) and promoted instead a mystical, pacifist asceticism later dubbed "Tolstoyism" by his followers. For a man so committed to peace, his final days were sadly turbulent. In the days preceding his death, his wife was forced to wait and sleep in an unused train car; he allowed her to see him only in his last hour.

WHAT OTHER
NOTABLES SAID

If you throw a rock into a pack of critics you are likely to hit one who, like Virginia Woolf, believes that Tolstoy is "the greatest of all novelists."[6] Woolf is in good company. C. S. Lewis also felt that Tolstoy's powers of description were something remarkable: "*War & Peace* is in my opinion the best novel...."[7] Lewis's other observations on the novel are so clear and precise that they are worth quoting at length:

> [In *War & Peace*] I have felt everywhere–in a sense–
> you will know what I mean–that sublime indiffer-
> ence to the life or death, success or failure, of the
> chief characters, which is not a blank indifference

---

6. Virginia Woolf, *The Common Reader* (South Australia: The University of Adelaide, 2015) ebook.

7. C. S. Lewis, *They Stand Together: The Letters of C. S. Lewis to Arthur Greeves, 1914–1963* (New York: Harper Collins, 1979), letter from Oct. 13, 1942.

at all, but almost like submission to the will of God. Then the variety of it. The war parts are just the best descriptions of war ever written: all the modern war books are milk and water to this: then the rural parts—lovely pictures of village life and of religious festivals in wh. the relations between the peasants and the nobles almost make you forgive feudalism: the society parts, in which I was astonished to find so much humour.... There are love-passages that have the same sort of intoxicating quality you get in Meredith: and passages about soldiers chatting over fires which remind one of Patsy Macan: and a drive in a sledge by moonlight which is better than Hans Andersen. And behind all these, and uniting them, is the profound, religious conception of life and history wh. is beyond J. Stephens and Andersen, and beside which Meredith's worldly wisdom—well just stinks, there's no other word.[8]

---

8. Lewis, *They Stand Together*, letter from March 29, 1931.

SETTING, CHARACTERS, AND PLOT SUMMARY

In a book with nearly 600 characters, a reader may well find himself lost at sea without doing a little homework. Russian names in particular offer a unique challenge, as Russian characters have three (or sometimes four) names: the first name, the patronymic, and the family name. A nickname, or diminutive, is often added to the mix.[9] The patronymic takes the place of our middle name and tells us who the character's father is. A patronymic ends in the suffix *-ovich*, or *-evich* ("son of"), or *-ovna* / *-evna* ("daughter of"). So, Andrei *Nikolaevich* is "Andrei son of Nikolai." The last name is a family name, similar to the surname in English (i.e., Andrei Nikolaevich *Bolkonsky*). Nicknames are often formed by adding *-sha* or *-ka* to a name (Natalia becomes *Natasha*).

---

9. The introductory material in the Oxford World's Classics edition of *War and Peace* is very helpful on this front.

I have organized most characters by family; only family members who play an important or recurring role in the story are listed. A character's most frequently used name is italicized. *The Oxford World's Classics edition of War and Peace* uses a similar organizational system.

- *Setting:* Russia between 1805 and 1812 (centered on the Napoleonic Wars)

- Count *Pierre* Kirilych Bezukhov (Pyotr, Petrusha): the illegitimate son of Count Kiril Vladimirovich Bezukhov and arguably the main character of the novel

The Rostovs:

- *Nikolai* Ilyich Rostov (Nicolas, Nikolenka, Nikolushka, Kolya, Koko): the eldest son of the elderly Count Rostov and another central character
- Natalia Ilyinichna Rostova (Natalie, *Natasha*): Count Rostov's eldest daughter and the central female character of the novel

The Bolkonskys:

- *Prince* Nikolai Andreyevich *Bolkonsky*: A retired, selfish, and cruel old general
- Prince *Andrei* Nikolaevich Bolkonsky (Andre, Andryusha): Prince Bolkonsky's son and a main character

- Princess *Marya* Bolkonskaya (Marie, Masha): Prince Bolkonsky's devout daughter

The Kuragins:
- Prince *Anatole* Vasilievich *Kuragin*: Prince Vasili's wild young son
- Princess Elena Vasilyevna Kuragina (*Helene*, Ele, Lyolya): Prince Vasili's promiscuous and ambitious daughter and, eventually, Pierre's wife

The Drubetskoys:
- Prince *Boris* Drubetskoy (Borenka): Anna's clever and ambitious son
- *Julie Karagina*: a wealthy heiress who marries Boris

- Mikhail Ilarionovich *Kutuzov*: the wise Russian general
- Alexander Pavlovich Romanov (*Alexander I*): Emperor of Russia
- *Napoleon* Bonaparte (Napoleon I): Emperor of France

If any book resists a simple plot summary it is *War and Peace*. Tolstoy himself clarified that, "It is not a novel, even less is it an epic poem, and still less an historical chronicle. *War and Peace* is what the author wished and was able to express in the form in which it is expressed."[10] So plotting the story feels a little like plotting the Old Testament. Even so, there are a few key narratives that hold the story together.

The book opens in 1805 in the fashionable St. Petersburg home of Anna Pavlovna. At the ensuing party we are introduced to several of Tolstoy's favorite targets: the fickle members of the Russian nobility who adopt each passing fad and believe that they, in their cleverness, have fully understood the momentous events and important characters of their time. We also meet two of the central characters in the story: Prince Andrei Bolkonsky and Pierre Bezukhov. Prince Andrei is a serious young nobleman, clear-headed, bored, conscious of his responsibility. In contrast to Andrei, Pierre acts much like a large child. He is the bastard son of the dying Count Bezukhov and soon to be one of the wealthiest men in the country. Shortly after the opening scene he goes out with several friends, gets roaring drunk, and ties a policeman to a bear cub before throwing both into a river (several commentators suggest Tolstoy modelled Pierre after his own life).

The Rostovs are the most stable and conventional family of the story. Count Rostov and his wife are Jane Austen-esque in their amiability and domesticity. They have two sons, Nikolai and the younger Petya, and a beautiful daughter, Natasha.

---

10. Leo Tolstoy, "Some Words About War and Peace," published in *Russian Archive*, 1868.

In one way or another this core cast of characters are quickly swept up in the looming war with Napoleon. Prince Andrei and Nikolai both join the army and are changed by the surreal nature of war. Andrei is wounded in the battle of Austerlitz and, as he lies on his back, is struck by his own insignificance in the face of the infinite. When Nikolai sees French soldiers charging at him for the first time he feels surprise rather than fear; "Who are they? Why are they running? Can they be coming at me? And why? To kill me? *Me* who everybody loves?" (p. 201).[11] Both Nikolai and Andrei, however, survive and go on to distinguish themselves in later battles.

Pierre, meanwhile, is unable to see the use in joining the army to fight in a war he does not understand. Instead, he has begun to take on the duties of a landowner after his father's death. Before long he is enticed into marrying the beautiful Helene who quickly reveals her hand as an ambitious and unscrupulous social climber. After Pierre challenges one of her lovers to a duel in which neither is killed, he is struck by the apparent futility of his life and begins a quest to find meaning and truth. He becomes a freemason and is initially awed and changed by the spiritual sense of brotherhood and purpose. Later on, however, he is disillusioned when he sees the freemasons guided by the same petty political and selfish motivations that steer his wife.

---

11. All quotes from *War and Peace* are taken from the Oxford World's Classics edition (New York: Oxford University Press, 2010).

Napoleon's first campaign against the combined forces of Russia and Austria is short-lived, and before long he and Tsar Alexander are not only at peace but friends. Andrei comes home only to see his young wife die giving birth to their son. Nikolai Rostov also returns home for extended periods to help his aging father manage their estate. In one of the most beautiful scenes of the book, Tolstoy describes an autumn wolf hunt. By evening Nikolai, Natasha, and Petya have made it to the house of 'Uncle', an old neighbor of the Rostovs, where they dance and sing late into the night. On the ride home Natasha tells Nikolai, "I know I shall never again be as happy as I am now" (p. 551).

After his wife's death Andrei falls in love with Natasha, but he tells her he must wait a year to marry in order to honor his father's wishes. They are separated during that time and Natasha is seduced by Helene's younger married brother Anatole. She breaks off her engagement with Andrei and is only barely prevented from a midnight elopement by her watchful friends. Natasha is crushed by the realization of her own treachery and foolishness. Pierre, still searching for meaning and estranged from his wife, visits Natasha to offer what confort he can and finds himself falling in love with her.

In 1812 the fight between Napoleon and the Tsar is renewed and Napoleon marches into Russia. Andrei and Nikolai are once again caught up in the machinery of war. The wise old General Kutuzov is appointed

Commander-in-Chief, but despite his best efforts the French army advances inexorably into the heart of Russia. When Princess Marya, Andrei's sister, realizes she must abandon the family estate at Bald Hills, she asks the local peasants to pack up the family's possessions. However, moved by some unintelligible folk instinct, they refuse to obey. Nikolai happens to be stationed nearby and when he learns of the princess's plight he comes to her rescue. When he sees Marya, Nikolai begins to fall in love.

The French army continues its advance and, after the battle of Borodino, in which Andrei is seriously wounded, it becomes clear that they will capture Moscow. As the Rostovs are preparing to flee, Natasha orders their servants to unpack all the family belongings in order to make room for wounded Russian soldiers. Unbeknownst to her, Andrei is among the wounded. He and Natasha are reunited and reconcile. However, Andrei's wounds are severe, and before long it becomes clear that he will die. The shared grief at his death, however, brings Natasha and Marya together as friends.

Pierre, meanwhile, has remained in Moscow. He runs into a burning house to save a child but is arrested after defending a women being robbed. Pierre is lined up to be shot alongside several other prisoners but is spared at the last minute. Afterwards, as he contemplates the uselessness and cruelty of the executions, we are told that Pierre's faith "in the right ordering of the universe, inhumanity, in his own soul and in God, had been destroyed" (p. 1041).

In captivity Pierre meets a peasant, Karataev, whom everyone calls "little falcon" and who, every night, prays, "Lord, lay me down as a stone and raise me up as a loaf!" (p. 1046). Pierre discovers in Karataev what he has been searching for: a person who lives as if every part of his life had meaning. Pierre is, once again, caught up in an existential revelation.

At this point Napoleon's army has looted Moscow and the city is burning. In one of the great twists of history the French become victims of their own success and Napoleon is forced to flee back to France before his army is completely destroyed by cold and starvation. Petya, Nikolai's younger brother, has now joined the army, but is killed in a moment of foolish courage. During the attack in which Petya is killed, several Russian prisoners are freed, among them Pierre.

In one of the final military scenes of the story, two French soldiers wander, starving, into a Russian camp. The Russian soldiers take pity on them, and, in exchange for a few songs, give them food. The scene is reminiscent of the Rostov's wolf hunt and ends as the stars begin "to disport themselves in the dark sky: now flaring up, now vanishing, now trembling, they were busy whispering something gladsome and mysterious to one another" (p. 1180).

When Pierre is freed, he learns that his wife has died. The story wraps of with the happy marriages of Nikolai to Marya and Pierre to Natasha. After plumbing the depths of history, Tolstoy ends with two surprisingly intimate and seemingly trivial scenes. In the first Pierre and Natasha talk alone after a lively evening with the Rostovs.

> Pierre: "I only wished to say that ideas that have great results are always simple ones. The whole of my idea is that if vicious people are united and constitute a power, then honest folk must do the same. Now that's simple enough."
>
> "Yes."
>
> "And what were you going to say?"
>
> "I? Only nonsense."
>
> "But all the same?"
>
> "Oh, nothing, only a trifle," said Natasha, smiling still more brightly. "I only wanted to tell you about Petya: today nanny was coming to take him from me, and he laughed, shut his eyes, and clung to me. I'm sure he thought he was hiding. Awfully sweet! There, now he's crying. Well, goodbye!" and she left the room. (pp. 1267-1268).

In the final scene Andrei's young son wakes up from a dream in which he and his uncle Pierre are leading an army. Tolstoy ends by foreshadowing the December Uprising of 1825, the event that sparked his research into the Napoleonic Wars, but there is also something grand and transcendent in the final words of the novel. Lying awake in the dark, the young boy thinks to himself,

"Mucius Scaevola burnt his hand. Why should not the same sort of thing happen to me? I know they want me to learn. And I will learn. But some day I shall have finished learning, and then I will do something. I only pray God that something may happen to me such as happened to Plutarch's men, and I will act as they did. I will do better. Everyone shall know me, love me, and be delighted by me" (p. 1269).

WORLDVIEW ANALYSIS

Two questions lie at the heart of *War and Peace*. The first is an old one and well-worn: is man really free? Are we really, as William Henley wrote, the captains of our fate and the masters of our souls? Tolstoy answers this question with a story, but it is a story into which the author himself frequently comes to muse alongside his characters. In this way he is both author and character, historian and subject; paradoxes that ultimately tie in to the answer he presents.

The second question, and one that is closely related, has to do with man's relationship to time. How is it that finite man can be aware of, and even interact with, the infinite? In wrestling with this question Tolstoy is in good company. Solomon himself, in Ecclesiastes, writes, "He has made everything beautiful in its time. Also He has put eternity in their hearts, except that no one can find out the work that God does from beginning to end" (Eccl. 3:11). Man is, as Job says, "of few days and full of trouble. He comes forth like a flower and fades away" (Job 14:1-2). Yet there is something in us that is built to last forever. T. S. Eliot gets at the same paradox in his poem *Little Gidding* when he writes, "Here, the intersection of the timeless moment / Is England and nowhere. Never and always." And then later: "A people without history / Is not redeemed from time, for history is a pattern / Of timeless moments. So, while the light fails / On a winter's afternoon, in a secluded chapel / History is now and England."[12]

Together these two questions drive the narrative of *War and Peace*. Can man act of his own free will, and is there a part of him that transcends his own time?

Tolstoy's answers to these questions are both very simple and very complicated. (As Pierre says, ". . . ideas that have great results are always simple ones.") To the question of man's finitude, Tolstoy answers, Yes; man is part of something greater. To the question of man's free will, Tolstoy answers, No; men are not free, at least in the sense that we normally mean. He explains that, in the same way that humanity once had to come to terms with a heliocentric solar system, despite the apparent contradiction to our eyes, "it is necessary to renounce a freedom that does not exist, and to recognize a dependence of which we are not conscious" (p. 1308). Tolstoy's answer is complicated in that, to make sense of such a counterintuitive (and, to

---

12. T. S. Eliot, *The Collected Poems and Plays, 1909-1950* (New York: Harcourt, Brace & World, 1952) 138, 144-145.

many, distasteful) answer, he must tell us a long and many-layered story.

Tolstoy answers these questions, at the most basic level, through how he treats his characters. As one critic writes: "There is a powerful tension in Tolstoy's work between persons and types, the particular and the general, freedom and laws. The quintessential Tolstoyan atmosphere is one in which highly particularized characters, with their hairy fingers and short lips, experience universal emotions that might easily be transferred from one character to another."[13] When describing the field hospital where the wounded Andrei is lying, Tolstoy writes, "One of the doctors came out of the tent in a bloodstained apron, holding a cigar between the thumb and little finger of one of his small bloodstained hands, so as not to smear it" (p. 872). Through this small gesture, typical of Tolstoy, we see in a minor character someone every bit as human as the heroes of the novel.

One of the clearest examples of this attitude comes in a chance encounter between Andrei and two peasant girls. Andrei is leaving the remains of his family estate when he sees the girls stealing plums. At first they hide behind a tree, but then, "Believing their danger past, they sprang from their ambush and chirruping something in their shrill little voices and holding up their skirts, their bare little sunburnt feet scampered merrily and quickly across

---

13. James Wood, "Movable Types: How 'War and Peace' Works," *The New Yorker* (Nov. 26, 2007).

the meadow grass" (p. 755). Tolstoy writes of Andrei that, "A new sensation of comfort and relief came over him when, seeing these girls, he realized the existence of other human interests entirely aloof from his own and just as legitimate as those that occupied him" (p. 755). Each person is as important as any other because we are all of us the same in relation to something greater, something infinite.

The great and infinite to which Tolstoy refers is most often symbolized by the sky. The two heroes of the novel, Andrei and Pierre, both look to the sky as they realize the meaning of life, and Tolstoy frequently draws our attention to the sky (or the stars) at particularly significant points in the story. After Andrei is wounded at Austerlitz he finds himself lying on his back: "Above him there was now nothing but the sky—the lofty sky, not clear yet still immeasurably lofty, with grey clouds gliding slowly across it. 'How quiet, peaceful, and solemn, not at all as I ran,' though Prince Andrei... 'How was it I did not see that lofty sky before? And how happy I am to have found it at last! Yes! All is vanity, all falsehood, except that infinite sky'" (p. 299).

Pierre also is drawn to the sky as he wrestles with the meaning of his life. After he has saved a French officer, Pierre looks first at the glow of Moscow as it burns and then up at a comet. "Gazing at the high starry sky, at the moon, at the comet, and at the glow from the fire, Pierre experienced a joyful emotion. 'There now, how good it is, what more does one need?' thought he" (p. 980). Later, after he has been captured and met the peasant Karataev, Pierre again looks heavenward: "Pierre glanced up at the sky and the twinkling stars in its far-away depths. 'And all that is me, all that is within me, and it is all I!' thought Pierre. 'And they caught all that and put it into a shed boarded up with planks!'" (p. 1098). Just as for Andrei, the sky is Pierre's window to eternity. And it is during his imprisonment that Pierre comes to realize his own powerlessness in the face of that eternity: "He had learned that, as there is no condition in which man can be happy and entirely free, so there is no condition in which he need be unhappy and not free. He learned that suffering and freedom have their limits and that those limits are very near together…" (p. 1140).

Although Pierre and Andrei have similar revelations, their conclusions are not entirely the same. In Andrei's mind, "To love everything and everybody, and always to sacrifice oneself for love, meant not to love anyone, not to live this earthly life" (p. 1056). As he dies Andrei becomes increasingly cold towards Marya and Natasha and even his own child. Pierre, in contrast, seems to grow more earthly. Even when Karataev is shot Pierre cannot help but be interested in the executioner as one of his fellow men: "Pierre looked at this soldier and remembered that, two days before, that man had burnt his shirt while drying it at the fire, and how they had laughed at him" (p. 1145). In this divergence of Andrei and Pierre we might, perhaps, get a glimpse of Tolstoy's own struggle between the tangible, present roles of husband and father and the future role of mystic and monk. Either way, it is clear that both Andrei and Pierre have come to a deeper understanding of life as they surrender their own wills to something greater.

Through such a treatment of his characters, Tolstoy's answer to the questions of man's place in the universe and his free will is one and the same: although each of us is unique as a person, we are, at the same time, part of something far bigger. We are human in the same way that every person is human, and therefore our existence and our choices are not discrete events within our control. As Tolstoy says in the epilogue: "As the sun and each atom of ether is a sphere complete in itself, and yet at the same time only a part of a whole too immense for man to comprehend, so each individual bears within himself his own aims and yet bears them to serve a general purpose incomprehensible to man" (p. 1224).

To drive his point home Tolstoy frequently interjects with his own criticisms of those who think they are in control. According to Tolstoy, even the great Napoleon, "who seems to us to have been the leader of all those movements—as the figurehead of a ship may seem to a savage to guide the vessel—acted like a child who, holding a couple of strings inside a carriage, thinks he is driving it" (p. 1085).

Tolstoy weaves this thought in more subtly as well. In Andrei's first combat Tolstoy speaks twice of an "invisible hand" and an "invisible power" orchestrating the battle (pp. 195, 197). As the armies are preparing to fight at Austerlitz, he writes, "Just as in a clock the result of the complicated motion of innumerable wheels and pulleys is merely a slow and regular movement of the hands which show the time, so the result of all the complicated human activities of 160,000 Russians and French—all their passions, desires, remorse, humiliation, sufferings, outbursts of pride, fear, and enthusiasm—was only the loss of the battle of Austerlitz…" (p. 274). Much later, when Natasha is attending the opera at which Anatole Kuragin begins to seduce her, she passes into a "state of intoxication" and imagines that she and the actress on stage are performing in the same play. And in the final scene of the book young Nikolai dreams of an army made up of cobwebs (p. 1268).

But Tolstoy does not just argue that men have no real control over their lives. He also does his best to show that this is actually a freeing reality. Perhaps the clearest example of this can been seen through Karataev, or, as he is know to Pierre and his fellow prisoners, "little falcon." Karataev is the embodiment of the sparrows Jesus speaks about in Matthew 10:29—those who do not fall to the ground apart from the Father's will. Andrei is struck by a similar thought as he dies, "The fowls of the air sow not, neither do they reap, yet your Father feedeth them" (p. 1055). According to Tolstoy, "Freewill is for history only an expression for the unknown remainder of what we know about the laws of human life" (p. 1305). But for him this does not mean that humans are soulless chessmen, moved by a distant God. Tolstoy's characters, from the singing Uncle to brave Petya are too dear and too personal to be simply gears. Tolstoy makes it clear that, in rejecting the idea of free will, he is not rejecting each individual's worth, uniqueness or responsibility. Rather, it is through our surrender to and acknowledgement of a divine power that we find true freedom and peace. In his decision to end *War and Peace* with the intimate conversation between Pierre and Natasha, Tolstoy is not suggesting that the smallest of our actions are as impersonal as the movements of an army, but that all actions are equally significant in the eyes of an infinite author.

QUOTABLES

1. "A Tsar is history's slave."

    ~ Narrator, p. 649

2. "It is possible to love someone dear to you with human love, but an enemy can only be loved by divine love."

    ~ Andrei, p. 989

3. "He had learned that, as there is no condition in which man can be happy and entirely free, so there is no condition in which he need be unhappy and not free. He learned that suffering and freedom have their limits and that those limits are very near together...."

    ~ Narrator, p. 1140

4. "For us, with the standard of good and evil given us by Christ, no human actions are incommensurable. And there is no greatness where simplicity, goodness, and truth are absent."

    ~ Narrator, p. 1152

5. "If we admit that human life can be ruled by reason, the possibility of life is destroyed."

           ~ Narrator, p. 1217

6. "As the sun and each atom of ether is a sphere complete in itself, and yet at the same time only a part of a whole too immense for man to comprehend, so each individual bears within himself his own aims and yet bears them to serve a general purpose incomprehensible to man."

           ~ Narrator, p. 1224

7. "Freewill is for history only an expression for the unknown remainder of what we know about the laws of human life."

           ~ Narrator, p. 1305

21 SIGNIFICANT QUESTIONS AND ANSWERS

1. The first words of *War and Peace* are in French, and French is spoken frequently throughout the novel by Russians. How does Tolstoy's use of French affect the novel?

   As Amy Mandelker points out in her introduction to *War and Peace*: "the astute reader will observe that a predilection for speaking French is frequently an indictment of character.... It is often the case that a character's decision to speak French implies a false, pseudo-literary, immoral or insincere communication...."[14] Mandelker also points out that, "Natasha speaks French only at one point in the novel: that is when, attending the opera, she emulates Helene and falls in with the social world of the Kuragins.

---

14. Leo Tolstoy, *War and Peace* (New York: Oxford University Press, 2010), xiii.

> She writes in French only once, when breaking her
> engagement to Andrei."[15]

2. Anna Pavlovna's salon is the opening scene of the story,
    and we return to it again several times over the course
    of the novel. What do the salon and its characters
    represent?

> The salon is a window into the vapid nature of
> Russian society. It is a game with arbitrary rules
> where inanity is rewarded. In the first scene Anna
> Pavlovna moves around the room, "As the foreman
> of a spinning-mill when he has set the hands to
> work, goes round and notices, here a spindle that
> has stopped or there one that has creaks or makes
> more noise than it should, and hastens to check the
> machine or set it in proper motion…" (p. 11). Later,
> she interrupts a conversation Pierre is having because
> "Both were talking and listening too eagerly and too
> naturally…" (p. 14).

3. Describe Pierre's character. Compare him to the other
    major characters.

> Pierre is, of the male characters at least, the most
> thoughtful and the most animated. While Andrei
> too searches for meaning in what he does, he has
> a much easier time detaching himself from those
> around him. Nikolai, while good natured and
> energetic, never digs much deeper than his own
> immediate desires. Pierre, however, puts his whole

---

15. *War and Peace*, xiv.

heart into everything he does. When we are first introduced to him he is described as "something too large" for Anna Pavlovna's drawing room. Pierre really is the largest character of the book.

4. Lewis and several other commentators point out how accurate Tolstoy's descriptions of war are. How does Tolstoy describe war?

Tolstoy describes war as an incredibly surreal experience, juxtaposing violence with the commonplace. For example, in one of the early scenes of combat, he describes a dam "over which for so many years Moravians in shaggy caps had peacefully driven their two-horse carts loaded with wheat and had returned dusty with flour," and over which men "now crowded together, crushing one another, dying, stepping over the dying and killing one another, only to move on a few steps and be killed themselves in the same way" (p. 308).

5. Describe Prince Bolkonsky. How does Prince Bolkonsky treat his children? Why?

Although Bolkonsky loves his children, he can only express that love through tyranny and, often, anger. He is always busy and very exacting. When we first meet him he is turning a lathe and surrounded by things "evidently constantly in use." He is particularly hard on Marya, but often his outbursts are followed by surprising tenderness. He is the most controlling character and also the most frustrated.

This ties in well with Tolstoy's claim that none of us can really direct our lives.

6. When Pierre attempts to free his serfs he is outwitted by his steward. Tolstoy describes the steward as "a very stupid but cunning man who saw perfectly through the naive and intelligent count" (p. 407). How could this be?

> This description is typical of the paradoxical way Tolstoy approaches his characters. Those who are viewed by society and history as great are often fools, while the simplest and humblest characters are the wisest. True intelligence lies not in a person's ability to get ahead, but in their willingness to recognize a power and purpose greater than themselves.

7. What do Pierre and Andrei discuss on the raft as they journey to Bald Hills? What happens to Andrei?

> They are discussing man's destiny and purpose and whether or not there is a life after death. Pierre is certain that there is and that man is part of some eternal whole, although he can't quite express what he means (he doesn't quite know himself). Andrei too believes in an afterlife, especially since the death of his wife, but is not so optimistic. Pierre points to the sky to illustrate his point and Andrei suddenly feels himself changed: "something that was best within him, suddenly awoke, joyful and youthful, in his soul" (p. 417).

8. Why is the old oak tree that Andrei notices important?

> The first time Andrei sees the tree it is standing
> old, gnarled, and bare in the early spring. It seems
> to say that, despite the new greenery budding all
> around, life at its core is hard and grim. When
> Andrei passes the tree a few months later, however,
> it is covered with leaves. This stirs in Andrei a new
> sense of purpose to live his life for those around
> him (p. 452).

9. What role does music play in the story?

> Music is often a sign of peace and a glimpse into
> eternity. It is as Natasha is singing that Andrei first
> falls in love with her and feels a "vivid sense of the
> terrible contrast between something infinitely great
> and illimitable within him, and that limited and
> material something that he, and even she, was" (p.
> 499).

10. There are only a few explicitly religious passages in the
    book. Around whom are they centered? Does Tolstoy
    treat this character as credible?

> Marya Bolkonskaya is the most explicitly devout
> of all the characters. When we are first introduced
> to her she is saying a prayer on the way to see her
> tyrannical father. Shortly afterwards she writes to
> her friend Julie that "Christian love, love of one's
> neighbor, love of one's enemy, is worthier, sweeter,
> and better, than the feelings which the beautiful
> eyes of a young man can inspire…" (pg. 101). Later,

we learn that Marya disobeys her father's wishes by welcoming in the poor whom Andrei mockingly calls 'God's folk.' It is unclear how far Tolstoy endorses Marya's devout orthodoxy, but she is certainly one of the more noble and consistent characters of the book and, along with Natasha, makes one of the happiest marriages.

11. Why does Pierre finally become disillusioned with the freemasons?

Pierre realizes that many of the freemasons either do not understand what they are doing or are only involved in the brotherhood for personal gain. When Pierre gives a speech urging his brothers to true reform and action he is reprimanded for causing strife.

12. How does Nikolai view his own courageous charge at Ostrovna?

Nikolai is surprised by the whole experience. He does not feel particularly brave and recognizes that his actions were not at all motivated by patriotism. In fact, he thinks mainly of the French officer he captured: "And how was he to blame, with his dimple and blue eyes? And how frightened he was! He thought I would kill him. Why should I kill him?" (p. 702).

13. How does Tolstoy view Napoleon?

> Tolstoy feels something between disgust and
> contempt for the French emperor. He describes
> Napoleon in animal-like terms: "Slightly snorting
> and grunting, he presented now his back and now
> his plump hairy chest to the brush with which his
> valet was rubbing him down…. 'Go on harder, go
> on!' he muttered to the valet who was rubbing him,
> slightly twitching and grunting" (p. 834). As far as
> Napoleon's reputation for military genius, Tolstoy
> pulls no punches. Napoleon's orders had nothing to
> do with the temporary success of his army, and, if
> they were carried out at all, only hindered his aims.

14. Explain the importance of Rastopchin's execution of
    Vereshchagin. What point is Tolstoy making?

> Rastopchin is both unjust and cruel when he makes
> Vereshchagin a scapegoat for the fall of Moscow.
> Tolstoy's description of the mob's fury is particularly
> graphic. When they are done they pull back, horri-
> fied, from his body, "with its long thin half-severed
> neck." Even Rastopchin begins to repent, but
> quickly justifies himself as all cowards do: it was for
> the good of others (p. 957). The whole scene brings
> to mind another famous coward handing over an
> innocent man to a murderous mob.

15. What does Andrei discover as he is lying in the field
    hospital with Anatole Kuragin?

    > As Kuragin is having his leg amputated, Andrei
    > recognizes him and is overcome with pity. Their
    > mutual proximity to death forces Andrei to see
    > Kuragin as a fellow man. Later, as Andrei approach-
    > es death, he thinks, "It is possible to love someone
    > dear to you with human love, but an enemy can
    > only be loved by divine love" (p. 989).

16. What strikes Pierre about Karataev? Why is he such a
    significant character in Pierre's development?

    > When they first meet, Karataev tells Pierre that
    > "things happen not as we plan but as God judg-
    > es" (p. 1044). Karataev is the first character Pierre
    > meets that really embodies this truth. He has come
    > to terms with the fact that he is an instrument of
    > God's will, and that fact has given him an outlook
    > on life that is both cheerful and steady. To Pierre
    > he is the "the eternal personification of the spirit
    > of simplicity and truth" (p. 1047). And because
    > Karataev can see that his whole life is in God's
    > hands, he also recognizes, as few other characters
    > do, that every part of his life is both connected and
    > important.

17. Describe the deaths of Petya and Karataev. How are
    they similar?

    > Both Petya and Karataev's deaths seem particu-
    > larly tragic: Petya's because the war had already

been won and he need not have entered the fight at all, and Karataev's because he had done nothing wrong. When Petya dies he describes how Denisov yelps like a dog. When Karataev is shot a dog begins to howl, and Pierre cannot force himself to meet his friend's last pleading look. The dogs serve to highlight both the intense, animal-like quality of grief, as well as the guilty stoicism of the soldiers who hurry away.

18. What does Tolstoy mean when he says, "If we admit that human life can be ruled by reason, the possibility of life is destroyed" (p. 1217)?

Human life is far too varied and complicated to be simply rational. None of us makes decisions, or submits to another's will, based purely on reason. If we did, we would be giving up an essential part of what it means to be human—not only our emotions, but those millions of barely conscious thoughts, hunches, and affections that influence every action we take.

19. Unpack young Nikolai's thoughts at the end of the novel.

Nikolai's dream and his thoughts afterward stem partly from the earlier conversation between his uncles and partly from his reading in Plutarch. Tolstoy's allusion to Plutarch serves as a good reminder that history has always followed the same rules. In his ambition to be like Mucius Scaevola,

> Nikolai is determined to join a cast of historical
> characters who have played their roles well.

20. In the final epilogue Tolstoy explains the problem that
    modern historians have created for themselves. What
    is it?

    > Tolstoy argues that by rejecting a Deity who
    > controls and orders history, modern historians are
    > forced to explain how individual men may lead
    > entire nations according to their single will, and
    > how a great number of people may even unify
    > their different wills towards the same end.

21. How does Tolstoy use the analogy of a ship to explain a
    common misconception about history?

    > Tolstoy argues that attributing historical cause to
    > the will of a particular character is like looking at
    > the wave created by the bow of a ship and as-
    > suming that the wave is leading the ship onward,
    > simply because it appears to precede it. Not only is
    > causation not a simple question of chronology, but
    > reducing any historical explanation to the will of
    > one man both misunderstands human nature and
    > ignores important factors which are entirely outside
    > of anyone's control.

FURTHER DISCUSSION
AND REVIEW

Master what you have read by reviewing and integrating the different elements of this classic.

SETTING AND CHARACTERS

Be able to compare and contrast the personalities (including strengths, weaknesses, and mannerisms) of each character. Which characters change over the course of the novel? Which do not?

PLOT

Be able to describe the beginning, middle, and end of the book along with specific details that move the plot forward and make it compelling. This includes the success or downfall (or both) of each character.

CONFLICT

Go through the character list and describe the tension between any and all main characters. Then, think about whether any characters have internal conflict (in their own minds). Is there any overt conflict (fighting), or conflict with impersonal forces?

THEME STATEMENTS

Be able to describe what this classic is telling us about the world. Is the message true? What truth can we take from the plot, characters, conflict, and themes (even if the author didn't believe that truth)? Do any objects take on added meaning because of repetition or their place in the story (i.e., do any objects become symbols)? How does the author use perspective, tone, and irony to tell the truth?

- Marriages make up a large percentage of the conflicts and relationships in the story. Marriage is one of the most tangible ways for people to transcend themselves through both space (another person) and time (children).

- At several points in the story characters find a kind of peace as they go to war, and some of the most violent and troublesome scenes are domestic. Clearly peace is not dependent on outward circumstances.

- Objects in the natural world—trees, rivers, ponds, stars—are often highlighted at significant turning points in the story. The everyday world around us is both eternal (God will raise up a new heaven and a new earth) and important (God calls his creation good).

Finally, compose your own theme statement about some element, large or small, of this classic. Then, use the Bible and common sense to assess the truth of that theme statement.

A NOTE FROM THE PUBLISHER:
TAKING THE CLASSICS QUIZ

Once you have finished the worldview guide, you can prepare for the end-of-book test. Each test will consist of a short-answer section on the book itself and the author, a short-answer section on plot and the narrative, and a long-answer essay section on worldview, conflict, and themes.

Each quiz, along with other helps, can be downloaded for free at www.canonpress.com/ClassicsQuizzes. If you have any questions about the quiz or its answers or the Worldview Guides in general, you can contact Canon Press at service@canonpress.com or 208.892.8074.

ABOUT THE AUTHOR

Samuel Dickison is a secondary teacher at Logos School in Moscow, Idaho where he teaches ancient history, literature, and rhetoric. He got his bachelor's degree at New Saint Andrews College, also in Moscow, and has taught fifth grade at Trinity Christian School in Kailua, Hawaii. He and his wife Rosalie have two children.

www.ingramcontent.com/pod-product-compliance
Lightning Source LLC
Chambersburg PA
CBHW071934020426
42331CB00010B/2867